# BigTime® Piano

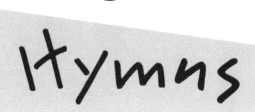
Hymns

T0086911

**Level 4**

**Intermediate**

This book belongs to: _____

**Arranged by**

**Nancy and Randall Faber**

Production: Frank and Gail Hackinson
Production Coordinator: Derek Richard
Editor: Edwin McLean
Cover: Terpstra Design, San Francisco
Engraving: Tempo Music Press, Inc.

# FABER
**PIANO ADVENTURES®**
3042 Creek Drive
Ann Arbor, Michigan 48108

# A NOTE TO TEACHERS

**BigTime® Piano Hymns** is a collection of favorite hymns and spirituals arranged for the Level 4 pianist. Keys include C, G, F, and D Major, along with D Minor. The teachers may assign the pieces in the order given or may skip among selections, choosing by student interest.

**BigTime® Piano Hymns** is part of the *BigTime® Piano* series arranged by Faber and Faber. As the name implies, this level marks a point of significant achievement for the piano student.

Following are the levels of the supplementary library, which lead from *PreTime®* to *BigTime®.*

| | |
|---|---|
| PreTime® Piano | (Primer Level) |
| PlayTime® Piano | (Level 1) |
| ShowTime® Piano | (Level 2A) |
| ChordTime® Piano | (Level 2B) |
| FunTime® Piano | (Level 3A – 3B) |
| BigTime® Piano | (Level 4) |

Each level offers books in a variety of styles, making it possible for the teacher to offer stimulating material for every student. For a complimentary detailed listing, e-mail faber@pianoadventures.com or write us at the address below.

Visit **www.PianoAdventures.com**

**Helpful Hints:**

1. Skillful pedaling is important in hymn playing. Pedal markings are provided in each piece. The student can benefit from practicing the left hand alone with attention to pedaling.

2. For a special project, the student may wish to record a selection of hymns and spirituals as a surprise gift for parents or grandparents.

3. Encourage students and parents to seek out opportunities for informal performances of hymns and spirituals, e.g., before or after a church choir rehearsal, for junior church service or Sunday School, or in a relaxed family gathering. Hymns are to sing and enjoy!

ISBN 978-1-61677-435-6

# TABLE OF CONTENTS

# It Is Well With My Soul

Music: Philip P. Bliss
Words: Horatio G. Spafford

# Come, Ye Thankful People, Come

Music: George J. Elvey
Words: Henry Alford

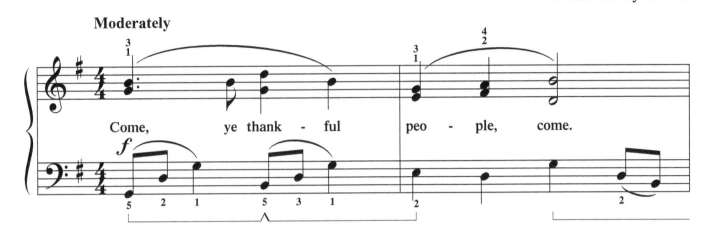

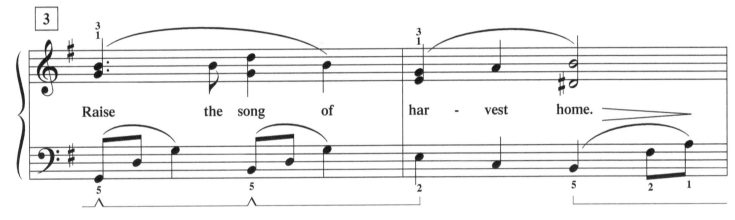

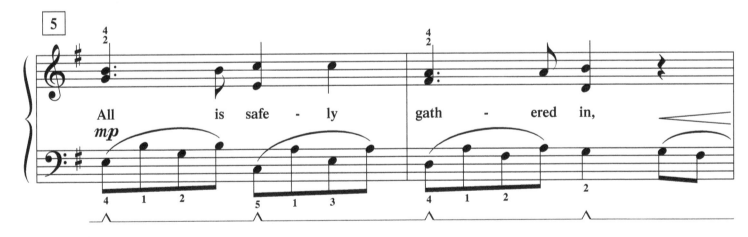

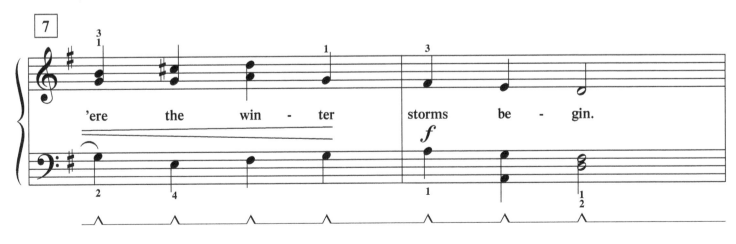

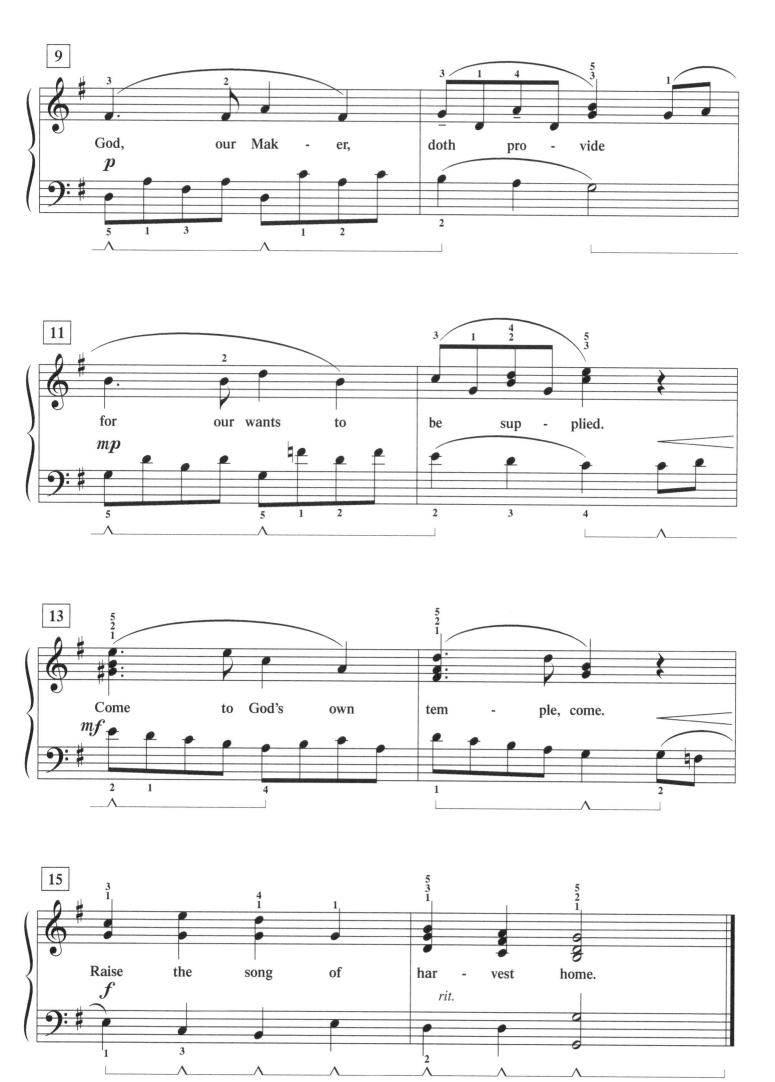

# Shall We Gather at the River

Robert Lowry

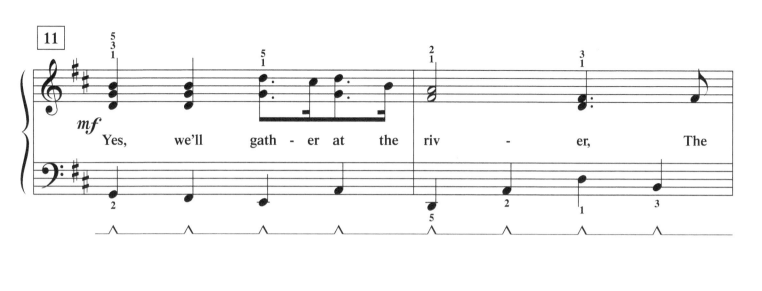

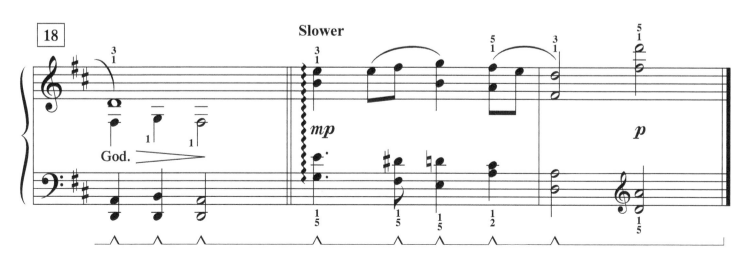

# Glorious Things of Thee Are Spoken

Music: Franz Joseph Haydn
Words: John Newton

FF1435

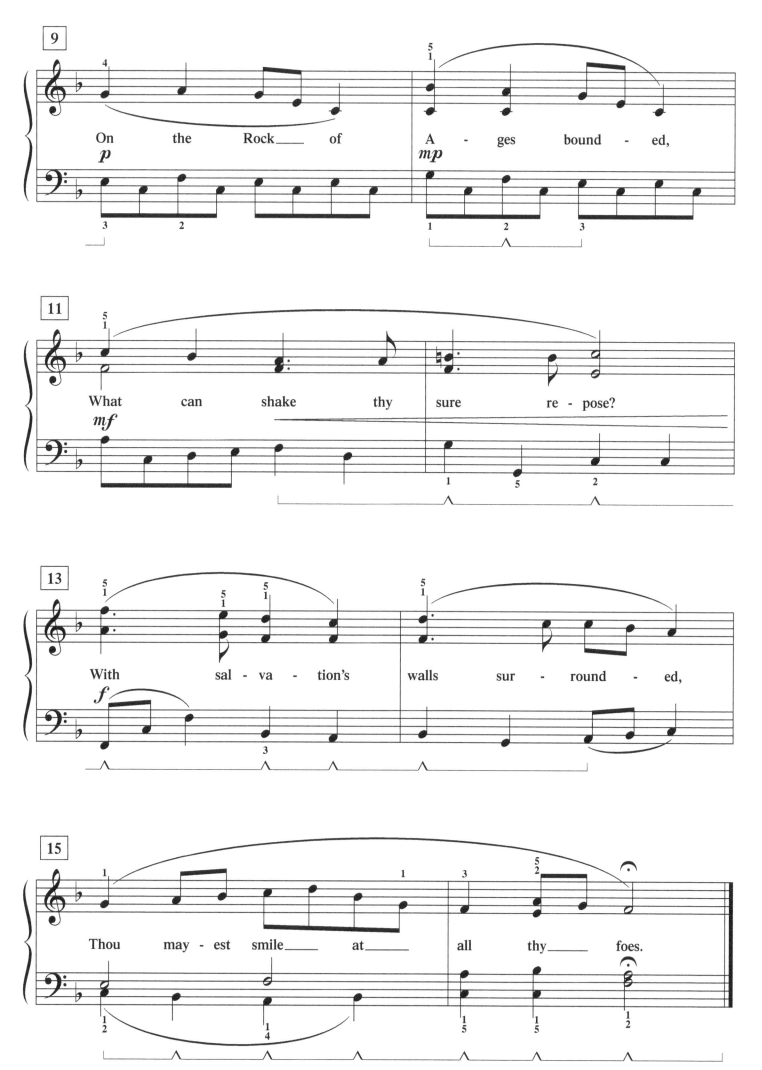

# Sweet Hour of Prayer

Music: William B. Bradbury
Words: William W. Walford

Gently

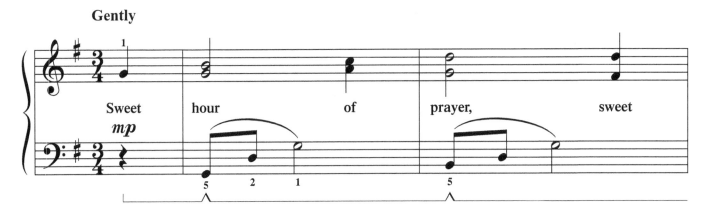

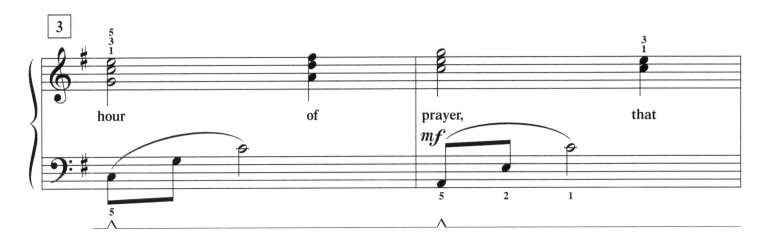

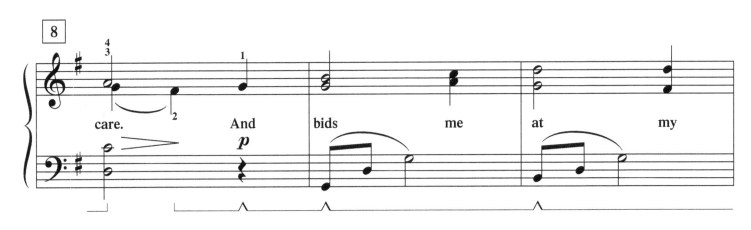

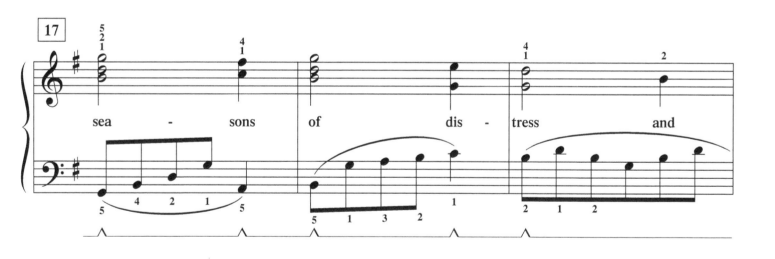

14

# The Old Rugged Cross

George Bennard

love       that  old       cross          where the    dear - est and

best,          for    a         world       of  lost        sin - ners  was

slain.                                      So  I'll    cher - ish the

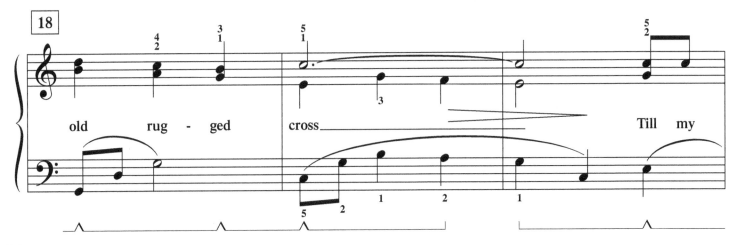

old    rug - ged    cross                           Till my

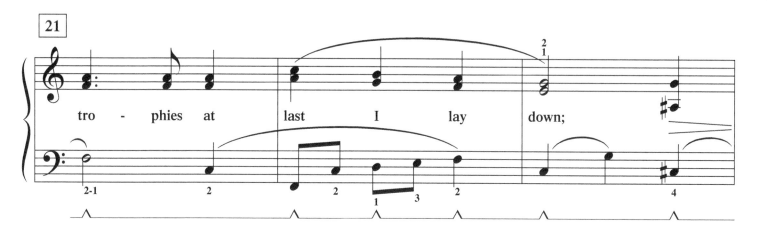

tro - phies at last I lay down;

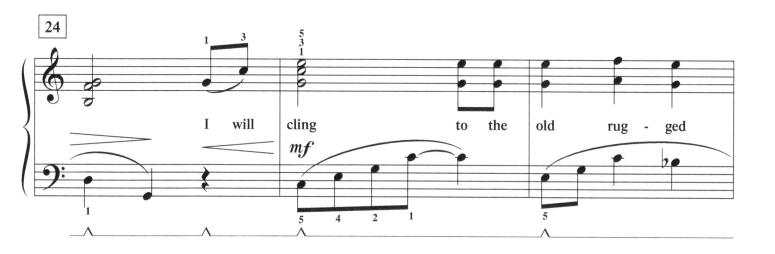

I will cling to the old rug - ged
*mf*

cross, And ex - change it some
*f*

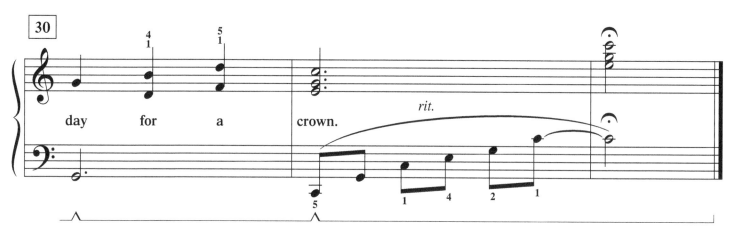

day for a crown.
*rit.*

# All Hail the Power of Jesus' Name

Music: Oliver Holden
Words: Edward Perronet

# Rock of Ages

**Music: Thomas Hastings**
**Words: Augustus M. Toplady**

# O Master, Let Me Walk with Thee

Music: H. Percy Smith
Words: Washington Gladden

se - cret, help me bear the

strain of toil, the fret of care.

*Fine*

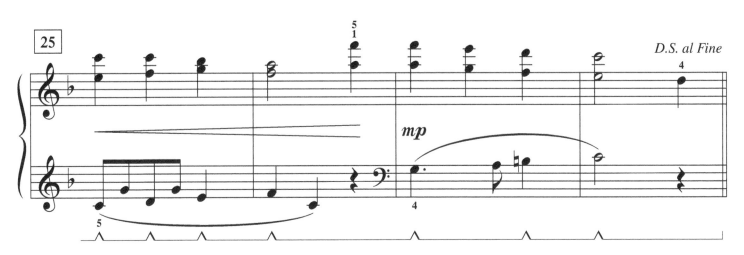

*D.S. al Fine*

# Break Thou the Bread of Life

Music: William F. Sherwin
Words: Mary A. Lathbury

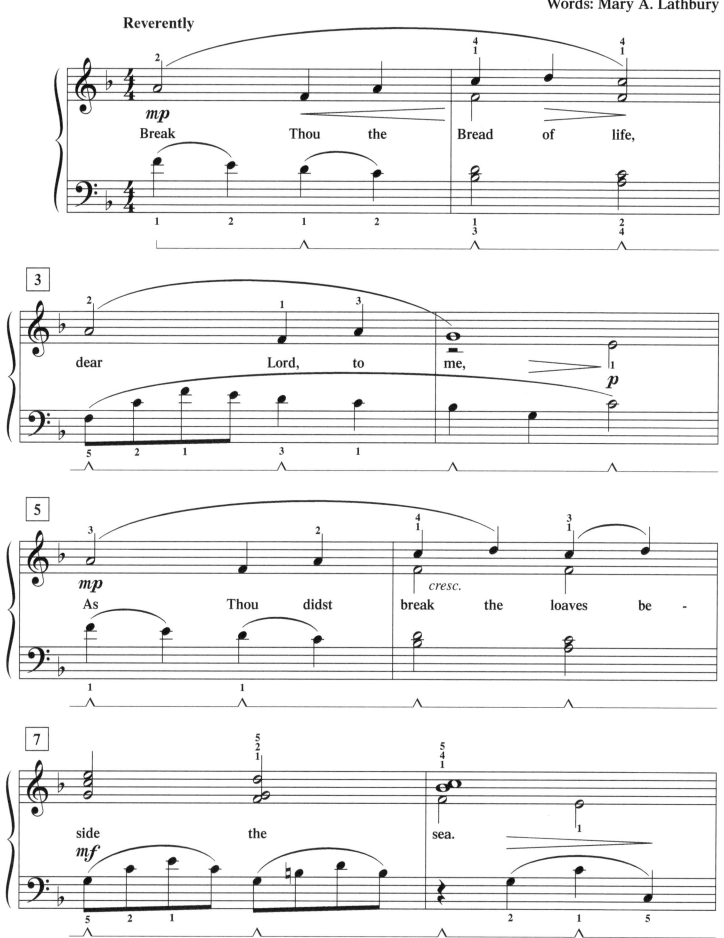

# Crown Him with Many Crowns

Music: George J. Elvey
Words: Matthew Bridges

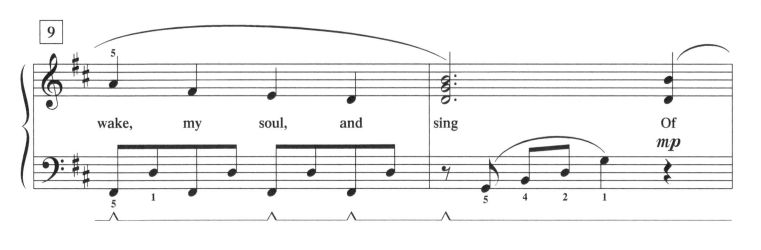

wake, my soul, and sing Of

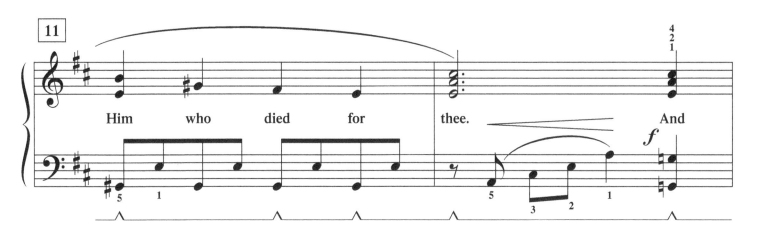

Him who died for thee. And

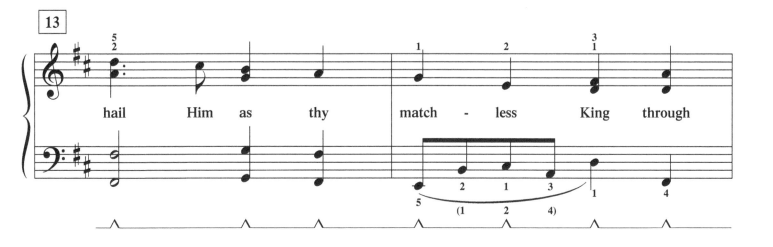

hail Him as thy match - less King through

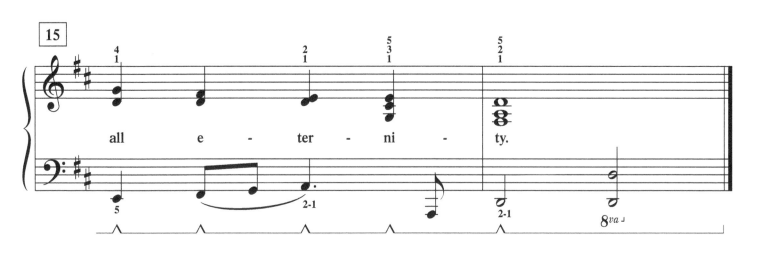

all e - ter - ni - ty.

# Jesus Shall Reign

**Music: John Hatton**
**Words: Isaac Watts**

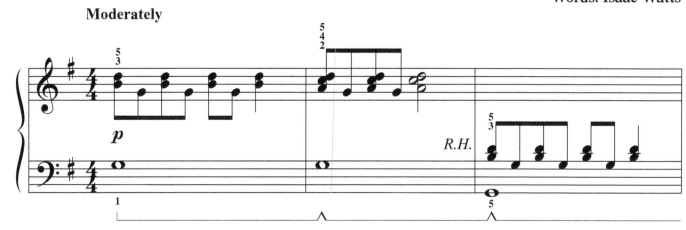

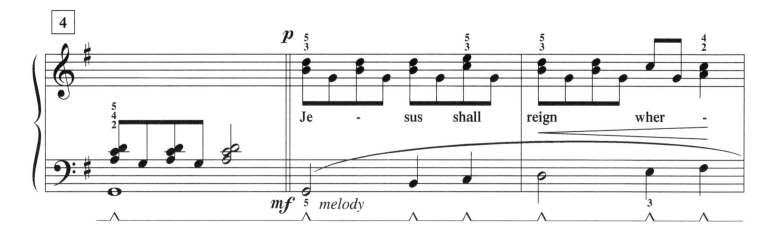

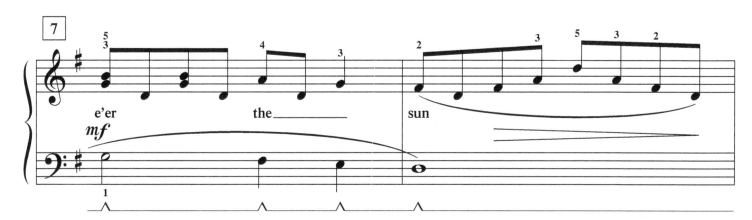

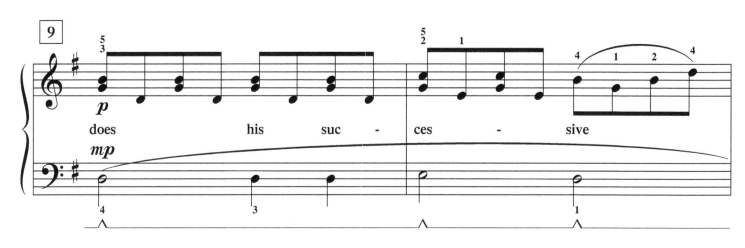

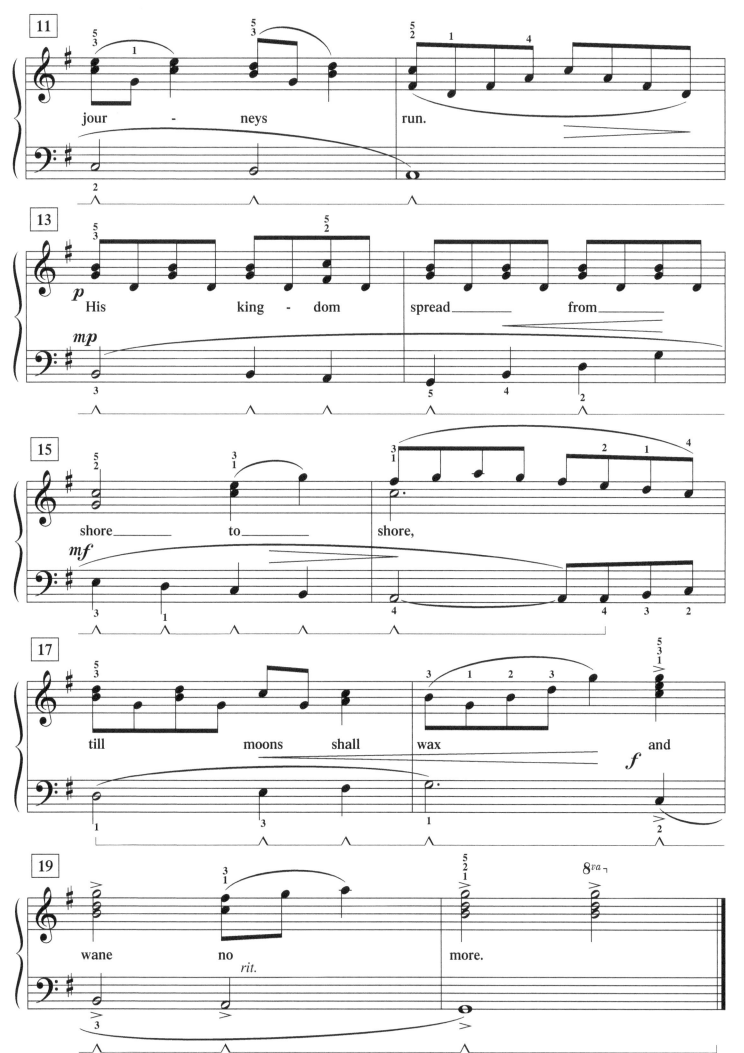

# Just As I Am

Music: William B. Bradbury
Words: Charlotte Elliott

# Deep River

Spiritual

FF1435

# A Mighty Fortress Is Our God

Martin Luther

# All Night, All Day

Spiritual

# Praise God, from Whom All Blessings Flow

Music: attributed to Louis Bourgeois
Words: Thomas Ken

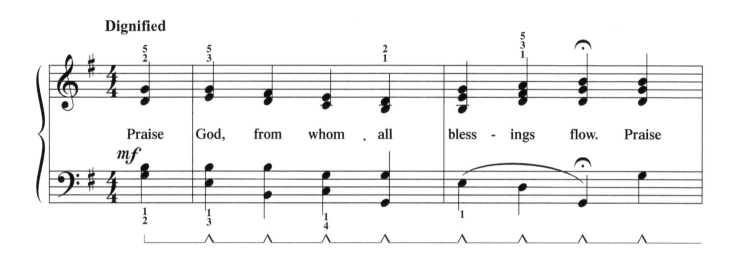

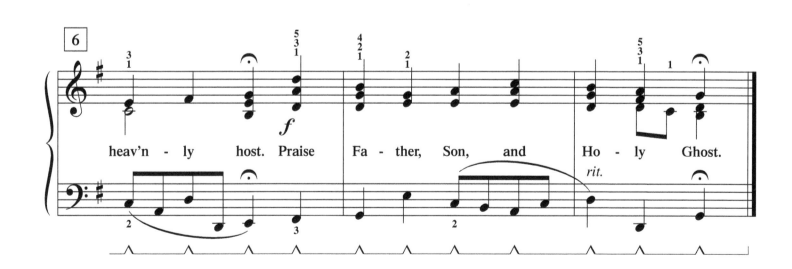